# Approved by LEO

The finest seal of approval based on taste, looks and durability. All done by my son Leo at 1,5 years old.

I0163241

## COPYRIGHTS

**Publisher:** Skyborn Works
**Ilustrations:** Simon Zingerman
**Typography:** Block Pro+, Knewave, FF Providence Sans and Interstate.
**OFL:** The font software Knewave is licensed under the SIL Open Font License, Version 1.1. Author: Tyler Finck, Copyright © 2010.

## ISBN

**ISBN-13:** 978-91-980904-3-7

## CONTACT INFO

Skyborn Works, Lyckselevagen 38, LGH 1102.
162 67 Vallingby. SWEDEN.
T: +46 73 649 83 11
contact@skybornworks.com

www.futurelittle.com
www.skybornworks.com

# DISC
# JOCKEY

# TURNTABLE

# VINYL RECORD

# HEADPHONES

LAPTOP

# SPEAKERS

# KEYBOARD

# MICROPHONE

# DIGITAL CONTROLLER

# MIXER

# RECORD COLLECTION

# NIGHTCLUB

# SCRATCHING

# SAMPLING

DJ MIX

# BPM

TEMPO

# AUDIO SOFTWARE

# REQUESTS

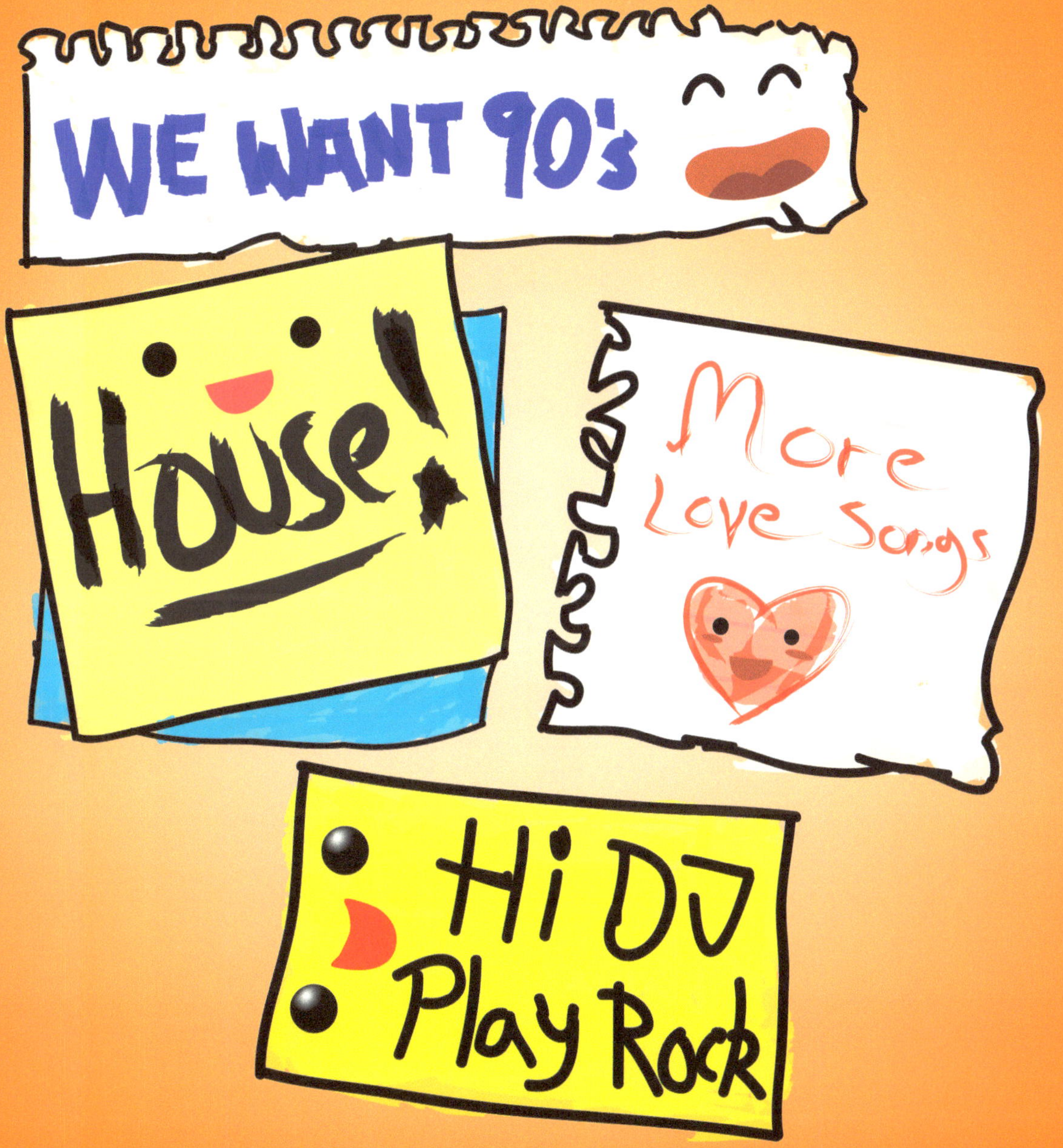
WE WANT 90's
House!
More Love Songs
Hi DJ Play Rock

# KNOBS

# FADERS

# DANCE FLOOR

# DANCE
# LIGHTS

www.ingramcontent.com/pod-product-compliance
Lightning Source LLC
Chambersburg PA
CBHW042059040426
42448CB00002B/73